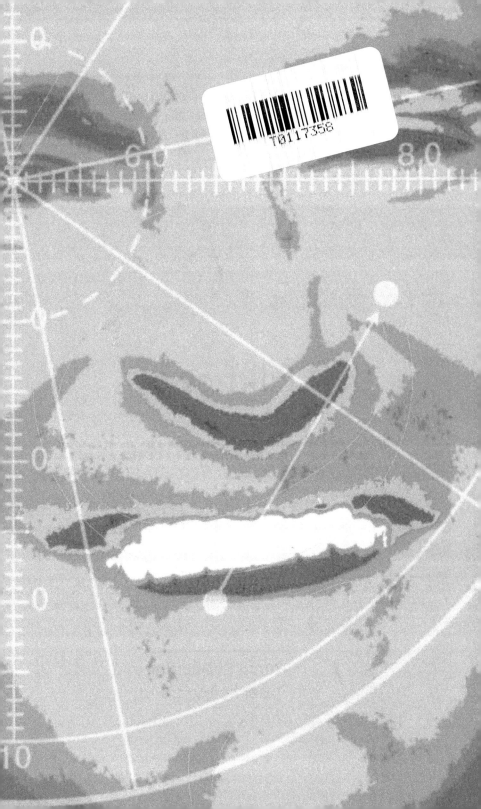

T0117358

Politics of

Self-Determination

Timothy Leary

Ronin Publishing
Berkeley, Ca

The Politics of Self-Determination

by Timothy Leary

ISBN: 1-57951-015-9; E-ISBN 1-57951-075-2

Published by

RONIN Publishing, Inc.

P.O. Box 22900

Oakland CA 94609

www.roninpub.com

Editor: Beverly Potter

Cover design: Judy July, Generic Typography

Printer: KNI Incorporated.

Printed in the United States of America

Distributed by Publishers Group West

Library of Congress Card Number - 00-103336

Some material in this book was previously published in *Changing My Mind Among Others* (1988) and *Chaos & Cyber Culture* (1994).

Homage to

Christopher Columbus, genius navigator, indefatigable scientist, whose optimism, courage, interpersonal skill and sense of genetic mission produced the New Worlds in which new visions, new cultures, and new intelligence could emerge.

Table of Contents

Foreword

By Dr. Beverly Potter

The name Timothy Leary brings LSD and his famous mantra, "Turn on, tune in, drop out," to mind. But few people know about the bedrock work that got him a Harvard appointment.

Even as a graduate student, Timothy had a swashbuckling, pushing the envelope attitude. Anyone who has been in a doctoral program will chuckle at his being an "intelligence agent." Timothy had high aspirations—to develop a theory of personality. If

> **Even as a graduate student, Timothy had a swashbuckling, pushing the envelope attitude.**

that weren't enough, he wanted to create a validated test to measure it. What is remarkable is that he actually succeeded in doing so—while still in graduate school.

The notion was to apply a nuclear physics approach to classifying human interactions. He talked about "human movements and collisions in space-time." Physicists use "cyclotrons" which are controlled environments where particles are studied, so Timothy proposed a *psychlotron* in which to observe, record and measure "human particles." Therapy groups served as his psychlotron. Today counseling groups are commonplace but back in the 1950s they were, in Timothy's words, viewed as "recklessly dangerous."

Such research was outside the boundaries of acceptability for graduate students. Timothy tells how he got around this barrier by enlisting two fellow students, and then going outside the department to obtain the sponsorship of a politics professor specializing in group dynamics.

This is the same strategy he employed years later at Harvard, where non-Md.'s conducting drug/brain research was unheard of. Not to be deterred, Timothy—always a ronin—again enlisted two cohorts, colleague Richard Alpert and then graduate student Ralph Metzner. He then went outside the academic and medical communities to the minister of a Unitarian church who agreed to sponsor a series of group counseling sessions for his congregation. In more recent times, Tom Peters, the business guru, touted a similar strategy, he called the "skunk works," for sliding around corporate boundaries to get things done without being immediately ejected.

Timothy's theory of personality is based on an interpersonal view in which we develop "interpersonal reflexes" to reduce social anxiety. Back in the 1950s, Timothy proclaimed: We are the masters of our lives and we create our own interpersonal reality—our *Preality*. Today we have a ho-hum attitude about this view, but back then this was pretty radical stuff! One can make a persuasive argument that Timothy's work was a significant catalyst that sparked and shaped the human growth potential movement—the so-called "New Age."

Years later in the Spring of 1970, after Timothy was so unfairly sentenced for having less than a full joint of marijuana, he was sent to Chino Prison where new prisoners were tested, interviewed, and classified to determine where they would be incarcerated for the long-term. The Gods were on his side:

Timothy reported to the psychological testing room. The official in charge smiled apologetically, "It seems we have a little problem here, Doc. The classification program here is partly based on psychological tests that you developed."

"That will teach me to mind my own business, " I said.

"We have to give you the tests. That's the rules."

"Let's go."

*The test of intelligence was to get the highest possible score. My answers to the personality tests were calculated to make me appear normal, non-impulsive, docile, conforming. My vocational tests revealed aptitudes in forestry and farming together with hopeless incompetence in clerical tasks. I was angling for a transfer to a minimum-security prison where escape would be possible.**

Timothy angled himself right into the California Men's Colony-West at San Luis Obispo where all he had to face was a "fifteen-foot barbed-wire fence and gun trucks manned by sharpshooters." Escape he did on Saturday, September 12, 1970. Timothy's description of the harrowing experience of a wimpy professor dragging himself along a twenty foot high mine cable—in full view of the gun trucks—while getting entangled in phone wires to cross the prison wall to freedom, where he was swept away by the Weathermen Underground—reads like a TV script. You can read the amazing tale in Timothy's autobiography, *Flashbacks.*

The first half of this book, which describes this early work, was mined from *Changing My Mind Among Others* published in the early 1980s. When I say "mined," I mean digging out nuggets lodged in disjointed, sta-

*From *Flashbacks: An Autobiography,* by Timothy Leary, Tarcher/Putnam, 1990.

tistical references and other incomprehensible language like: "In psychology, the classic polarity of inner-subjective and out-objective can be solved in the same way as in the physical sciences: through a continuum of visibility that runs from nuclear-particle behavior to chemical-molecular to microscopic to macroscopic." It was stultifying—definitely not reader friendly! I joked with my friends that I was channeling Tim—and maybe I was!

The book emerged from cutting and rearranging. Of course the statistical stuff was tossed out first. Paragraphs were moved around again and again. It was a little like gazing into a rippled pond with a reflection of Timothy's little book slowly emerging as the water stilled.

When Sebastian, my partner, and I were establishing Ronin Publishing, I was writing a book called *The Way of the Ronin*, which was published in 1984 by AMACOM—the American Management Association—the same year Ronin was incorporated. *Ronin* is a Japanese word that translates *ro* for waves and *nin*, like ninja, for man or person and refers to the so-called "masterless samurai" from feudal times who was thrown into the waves of a difficult and uncertain destiny. Samurai—who were a lot like our academically affiliated PhDs—without a master had to become *self-mastering*.

I like to say ronin were unindentured because samurai were actually chattel or property—yes, high class—but chattel nonetheless. They received a rice allowance and had nothing of their own. If one's master was disgraced and had to commit *seppuku*, his family and samurai were expected to cut out their own bowels along side of him. Any samurai who refused became a ronin.

Feudal Japan was rigidly structured and it was difficult for such an unaffiliated person to survive. When the bushi master said "Go and do ronin," it was a challenge of self-determination, of struggling with being an individual, standing apart against treacherous odds. Everyone in feudal Japan was forced into rigid conformity except the ronin—who were free. Have sword; will travel. They broke with convention and taught merchants and artisans how to use the special techniques of the long sword and the short sword. Essentially, *The Way of the Ronin* is about being a self-directed warrior-type person functioning excellently, by a personal of conduct, in a rigid, stupid system that wants to squelch your spirit.

The ronin archtype was a tuning fork to which we both resonated. Timothy, gotten a hold of a copy of *The Way of the Ronin* and called to rave about it. That's how we met. Little did I realize at the time the degree to which the ronin archetype was a tuning fork to which we both resonated. Tim quoted the book in a provocative article about cyberpunks and self-determination that came out in the *Mississippi Review* in 1988. That article shows how his thinking about self-determination had evolved by the end of his career and is included in this book.

I am amazed to realize how much I have in common with Timothy Leary. Much, undoubtedly is a reflection of the vast influence he had on my generation. After all, I was a hippie. I lived in the Haight-Ashbury during the Summer of Love. I went to the Love-In (also called the Human Be-In) where Tim proclaimed to a throng of psychedelized hippies:" Turn on, tune in, drop out." I was there! But I wasn't "into" Leary and never considered myself to have been particularly influenced by him.

The parallels go deeper. Timothy was a psychologist; I am a psychologist. Timothy's early work was with prisoners; my early work was with prisoners. Timothy worked with groups and, as a doctoral student, co-created a model of behavior in groups; I worked with groups and, as a doctoral student, co-created a model of behavioral group counseling. Timothy went to Berkeley; I went to Stanford—archrivals but in the same game. Timothy was a smart aleck upstart and so was I—still am. Timothy was a libertarian; I am a libertarian—the only one registered in my Berkeley prescient, by the way. Timothy believed in individual responsibility; I believe in individual responsibility. Timothy became associated in people's minds with psychedelics, which overshadowed his core work; I've become associated in many people's minds with Ronin's psychedelic books and few people know of my core work. Curious. With all these parallels one could argue that I'm uniquely suited to rebirth Timothy's work in *Politics of Self-Determination*.

This little book is an overview of Timothy's work in self-determination at the beginning of his career and at the end. Nestled here and there are glimpses of the attitudes that propelled him, and the strategies he used to get around the system to pursue his research.

Politics of Self-Determination is launching Ronin's Self-Mastery Series. Who better to do so than Timothy Leary who enjoined us to "Think for yourself," "Question authority," and "Just Say Know"? Enjoy folks!

—docpotter
April 2000

The Cyberpunk Code:

- Think for yourself
- Question Authority
- Just Say Know

Chapter 1

A Radical Proposal

I decided to become a psychologist in 1941, at age 21, because at that time, the profession appeared to be the sensible, scientific way of dealing with the classic human predicaments of boredom, ignorance, suffering, and fear.

To my young mind, it seemed logical that there could be no political-economic-spiritual solutions that were not based on the dramatic raising of enthusiasm, human, intelligence, guilt-free happiness and individual self-confidence.

Intelligence Agent

I served as a consultant psychologist in the US. Army Medical Corps from 1943 to 1946 and after the war enrolled as a graduate student at the University of California at Berkeley—which at the time was considered to have the best psychology department in the country, meaning it was the best in the world. For the first two months of graduate school, I performed routine tasks of surveillance—sitting in on lectures of top professors, surveying their publications, collecting graduate school gossip which is always the best source of information for an intelligence agent.

It was immediately apparent that the men who ran the Psychology Department were obsessed with minutiae of animal maze-learning—the analogy between students and rats was too painful to discuss openly—and uninterested in any experimentation on human behavior. They especially steered clear of research aimed at helping people or changing behavior. These genial academicians had spent twenty years attaining acceptance and status by committing themselves to one or another theory of animal learning, however irrelevant they were to the fast-changing realities in the outside world.

Clinical Psychology Was Hip

There was, however, a new branch of "clinical" psychology which, benefiting from an enormous influx of federal money set up ambitious programs to train graduate students in the diagnosis and treatment of human pathology. Later we learned that that cash fix was CIA inspired.

Anyone identifing hirself in a social situation as a "psychologist" received a visible, delicious shudder of anticipatory fear.

The conservative animal experimenters sagely complained that "clinical training" was simply teaching psychologists to become junior psychiatrists. Given the postwar prestige of Freudian psychoanalysis, however, even this subordinate association with the "couch mystique" was a matter of prestige to young psychologists, like myself.

As an anthropological aside, back in those days (1940 to 1959) anyone identifing hirself in a social situation as a "psychologist" received a visible, delicious shudder of anticipatory fear: "Oooh, can you look within and spy my secrets?" Today with 10s of 1000s of Ph.D.'s a year rolling off the assembly lines, the term "psychologist" elicits bored expectations of flaky self-importance. In the 1950s as portrayed by Woody Allen, "psychology" touched the same awe-change-magic that the word "drug" touched in later decades.

The Grand Ritual

Graduate interns in clinical psychology in 1946 were assigned to clinics and hospitals, where they gave diagnostic tests and participated in the Grand Ritual of the Staff Conference—which interested me in that it was the High Mass of the New Religion and clearly reflected its preoccupations. At the head of the table sat the chief psychiatrist, flanked on either side by subordinate members of the Medical Caste. Next came the Ph.D. psychologists.

The level of jargon was bizarre-baroque Freudian.

At the bottom of the table clustered the Psychiatric Social Workers—usually females. As social workers were permitted to do psychotherapy in the 1960s, 70s and 80s, thereby gaining prestige, men flocked to their ranks.

The Case

The "case" was presented. First the social worker spelled out the "patient's" social history. The psychologist then read his diagnostic testing report. In those cases where a psychiatrist had seen the "case," he contributed his impressions. Then, after a general discussion of the "case," the chief psychiatrist would pronounce a diagnosis and an administrative decision would be made about the patient: type of treatment, transfer to another ward or institution, discharge. The level of jargon was bizarre-baroque Freudian.

My first reactions of disbelief were followed by acute boredom. I sublimated my outrage with satirical remarks that made everyone laugh. After that, I often used humor as a tool to provide relativistic perspective.

> **I saw then that the success of a psychiatrist or clinical psychologist was in inverse proportion to the time spent in face-to-face interaction with the patient**

In time my boredom turned to phobic despair. It was clear that few had much interest in the patient's point of view. The unfortunate being called the "case" was treated as an abstraction around which whirled the most kinky sort of projections. Staff members routinely projected the contents of their own minds on the patient. In time, I saw the words of each clinician as strings of taffy emerging from their mouths and covering the table, the floor, and sometimes threatening to engulf the room. I impatiently longed for something tangible, measurable, real—to replace the speculation.

I saw then that the success of a psychiatrist or clinical psychologist was in inverse proportion to the time spent in face-to-face interaction with the patient. The most prestigious and well-paid professionals spent the least time with patients and devoted the majority of their time to administration, consultation, and supervision in their offices.

It followed that if one wished to learn about the laws of human behavior, it was necessary to spend no time in administration and devote all one's time out there in the field, on the street, on the front lines. Since having that insight, I tried to avoid having an office—and I was largely successful in doing so.

Chapter 2

The First Psychlotron

During this early introduction to clinical psychology, I came to the conclusion that human behavior should be studied in the same way physicists study the behavior of atomic particles. By contrast, Freudian orthodoxy operated with the 19th Century Newtonian Thermodynamic engineering view of human personality.

To understand the behavior of human individuals, I believed it was necessary to imitate the research techniques of 20th Century nuclear physics to create environments—cyclotrons—where human "particles" could be observed, recorded, and measured.

A psychlotron is an environment, where human behavior is intensified, accelerated, charged with high-voltage—where the social molecular structures are dissolved so that the individual's behavior and the conclusions and interactions can more easily be observed and recorded.

From that point on I was instinctively drawn to psychlotron places—high energy, high risk frontiers where human atoms are stripped from social bonds, free to operate according to internal gyroscopes interacting in clearly visible collisions with other free-spinning individuals.

In 1947, a medically trained psychiatrist considered group therapy as recklessly dangerous as requesting patients to perform perilous surgical operations on each other.

In my second year of graduate school, therefore, I used standard primitive political tactics to establish a psychlotron. I went to a popular political professor who specialized in group dynamics and asked him to sponsor a research project in the objective measurement of behavior of "patients" in groups.

Radical Research

To do this radical research without medical supervision and outside the clinical environment was the exact political difficulty we faced twelve years later when we began to research drugs at Harvard without medical degrees. And as with the Harvard research, I solved this problem by finding a valuable ally outside the academic or medical communities—Dr. Raymond Cope, Minister of the Berkeley Unitarian Church. In response to the common sense practicality and good will of my proposal, he enthusiastically agreed to sponsor a series of group counseling sessions for members of his student congregation.

After getting my professional support lined up, I purchased a wire recorder—this was before tapes were invented—enlisted the collaboration of two other graduate students and organized six counseling groups.

Looking back on it, it is hard to realize how eccentric and even illegal this was. We had essentially set up our own ad hoc clinic in which graduate students, on their own time, were "treating" 48 "patients" using a wildly radical technique—group therapy! In 1947, a medically trained psychiatrist considered group therapy as recklessly dangerous as requesting patients to perform perilous surgical operations on each other. In those primitive times, the unconscious was considered a primeval swamp of festering insanity.

In those primitive times, the unconscious was considered a primeval swamp of festering insanity.

Meanwhile we collected hundreds of hours of wire spools, which were transcribed by secretaries paid out of our graduate-student fellowship stipends.

Chapter 3

Behavior Trails

Following the modern physics metaphor, we considered each statement of each patient as a "behavior trail" analogous to that of an electron in a cloud chamber. Our aim was to classify these interactions in the same manner that nuclear physicists categorize the behavior of colliding particles, i.e., in terms of spatial coordinates: above or below, and positive/attraction or negative/repulsion. With this guiding standard, each statement of a patient was coded as to its effect of *putting down* or *elevating* the other person, and to its *affilative* or *hostile* effect.

After several weeks, the validity of the scheme became obvious. We were able to code human interpersonal behavior reliably in terms of a two-dimensional grid. We were charting objectively recorded human interactions the same way a naval radar operator could track the movement of ships.

Set and Setting

What a person does in any social situation is a function of at least two factors. First is "set" which is hir multilevel personality structure. Second is "setting" which are the activities and effect of the "other" person with whom one is interacting. The interpersonal meaning of any behavior can be determined by asking, "What is this person doing to the other? What kind of a relationship is the person attempting to establish through this particular behavior?"

The answers to these questions define the subject's interpersonal impact. For example, "She is boasting and attempting to establish superiority." Or, "He is rejecting and refusing to help." A father may employ one or 1,000 words to refuse his child's request. The mode, style, and content of his expressions may be very different, but their interpersonal effect—rejection—is the same.

Attitude Operationalized

We had made objective and scientific the classic ghost-in-the-machine of human psychology—Attitude. We could now define attitude, in the interpersonal context, as the angle of approach of another person.

We three graduate students had a vision of developing a theory of personality. With a Kaiser Foundation research grant we set out to study the "interpersonal core of personality."

> **We had made objective and scientific the classic ghost-in-the-machine of human psychology— Attitude!**

To this end a wide assortment of raw interpersonal data was assembled. Several scores of individuals—male and female, neurotic, psychosomatic, and normal—were brought into interpersonal relationships in small groups. Some of these were discussion groups in a non-psychiatric setting. Some were psychotherapy groups in an outpatient clinic.

Hundreds of interaction of each subject were observed, recorded, and studied. Many other types of verbal descriptions of self and others—present, past, and anticipated—were collected from expressions made in the groups or summaries in autobiographies and psychological inventories. The subjects dreams and fantasies were recorded. Their responses on batteries of projective tests were elicited.

Following the modern physics metaphor, we considered each statement of each patient as a "behavior trail" analogous to that of an electron in a cloud chamber.

A rich but unwieldy collection of raw material—in the form of wire recording spools, typed transcriptions, ratings, observers' reports, test indices, projective responses—piled up for each subject.

Rating Interactions

Our working principle held that the basic data of personality are not the raw responses but the units of protocol language by which the subject's interpersonal behavior can be summarized.

In rating, the observed and recorded interactions, we noticed that transitive verbs were the handiest words for describing what the subjects did to each other, e.g., *insult, challenge, answer, help*. In rating the content of the spoken or written descriptions of self-or-other, we noted that adjectives were more often suitable. Here we were interested in the attributes, qualities, and traits which the subject assigned to himself and others. "I am *friendly, helpful, strong;* they are *hostile, selfish, wise, helpful.*"

A clear relationship seemed to exist between these two types of interpersonal descriptions, such that the adjectives seemed to express an interpersonal attribute or potentiality for action, which the verbs described the action directly.

Three rather interesting notions began to develop out of this fact. First, the relationships between different expressions of personality can be directly related to each other by grammatical or linguistic procedures. That is, what you actually do in the social situation as described by a verb (e.g., *help*) can be related to your description of yourself (as described by the attribute *helpful*) and to your description of your dream-self or fantasy-self (also attributive, *helpful* or perhaps *unhelpful*). These grammatical relationships become key to a systematic consideration of the levels of personality.

Dominance and Affection

When dominance-submission was taken as the vertical axis and hostility-affection as the horizontal, all of the other generic interpersonal factors we had isolated could be expressed as combinations of these four nodal points.

The various types of nurturant behavior appeared to be blends of strong and affectional orientation towards others. Distrustful behaviors seemed to blend hostility and weakness. Further experimentation and review of the raw data led to the conclusion that a circular two-dimensional continuum of sixteen generic variables represented the optimal degree of refinement of interpersonal themes which we affectionately called our "Interpersonal Compass".

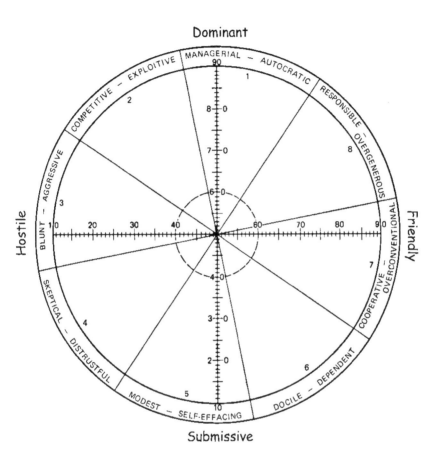

The Interpersonal Compass

Chapter 4

Interpersonal Compass

The four quadrants of the interpersonal system comprise blends of the nodal dichotomies: love versus hate and power versus weakness. The four "blended" quadrants fit rather closely the classical humors theory of Hipprocrates. The upper left quadrant—*hostile strength*—equates with the choleric temperment, the lower left—*hostile weakness*—with the melancholic, the lower right—*friendly weakness*—with the phlegmatic, and the upper right—*friendly strength*—with the sanguine.

By the way, the same fourfold classification reappears in Freudian thought. Freud's treatment of the individual stresses two basic motives—love and hate. His theories of social phenomena and group interaction, on the other hand, emphasize domination, power, and the interaction of the weak versus the strong.

Multilevel Interpersonal Diagnostic

Once we had established the compass points of a human interpersonal behavior, it was a simple matter to develop questionnaires that allowed therapists, diagnosticians, observers, even patients to describe their behavior in the same precise, calibrated language: "Patient X moved three points north (i.e. toward domination) in response to the therapists southeast approach."

Breakthrough

A breakthrough in human psychology was involved here. For the first time, interpersonal behavior of humans could be measured as objectively as nuclear-particle behavior, and in terms of the basic parameters-spatial relationships.

Treating "words" as emissions, the frequency and variety of which were of crucial importance to a "word-manipulating species," followed Zipf as a breakthrough in nuclear or particle psychology.

Worthy of historical note is that use of "multilevel" was not new. Freud had lifted this notion from Fliess and the German Romantics in the late 19th Century, but "measurement" as a psychological concept was alien to Freudians.

Every word on the Interpersonal Check List was "measured" in a series of computer studies. These words, when emitted from a test-subject, turned out to be highly predictable "particles." If you checked yourself as being "helpful" on this list, it was possible to predict with high probability how you would check any other word. Treating "words" as emissions, the frequency and variety of which were of crucial importance to a "word-manipulating species," followed Zipf as a breakthrough in nuclear or particle psychology. Another innovative contribution is the discussion of variability-changeability as an important dimension of human behavior.

For the first time, we could speak of Particle Psychology or Nuclear Psychology—a psychology comparable to physics in that both disciplines study the movements of particles. In the next 30 years, by 1979 the concept of personality classification in terms of one's own movements had led to such powerful concepts as swarming, population genetics, gene-pool migration, spin.

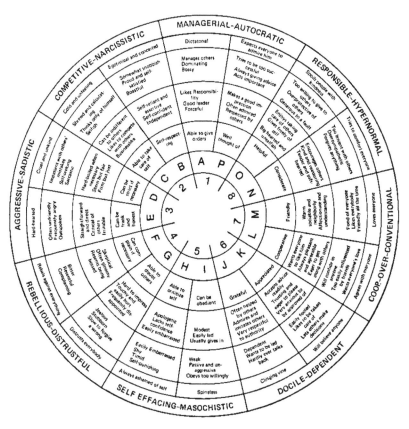

Interpersonal Wheel

We created a manual for using the Multilevel Interpersonal Diagnostic—which was produced by four intelligent women who were nonprofessional high school graduates. Here was another prelude to the "humanistic" sixties in which the trade-union monopoly of the professional psychologist-psychiatrist was broken-and everyone was challenged to become hir own life-doctor.

It Was a Hit!

We three doctoral students' radical research generated considerable interest. A new psychiatric clinic, connected with Kaiser Hospital in Oakland, California, built our interpersonal diagnostic tracking methods into its operation. By 1957, thousands of patients had been diagnosed and treated using these approaches. Hundreds of clinics and research stations as far away as Czechoslovakia and Israel were using these methods. Even our own CIA had adopted them. Dozens of scientific papers confirmed that the Interpersonal Compass was calibrated correctly—that human interpersonal interactions could be charted as objectively as nuclear particle collisions—and that such behaviors were of basic importance in human transactions.

In 1958, the experiments performed at the Kaiser Psychological Research Foundation involving millions of recorded interpersonal particle collisions were summarized in my book *Interpersonal Diagnosis of Personality*. The next year the *Annual Review of Psychology* called this "the most important book on psychotherapy of the year." In fact, it was the ground-breaking work that was largely responsible for getting my Harvard appointment.

Chapter 5

Principle of
Self-Determination

The principle of self-determination as first presented in *Interpersonal Diagnosis of Personality* was an important lurch in my evolution as a scientist. It was an amazing forecast of what I would be writing 25 years later—and, more to the point, a precise forecast of what best-selling prophets of the Sartrian me-generation would be saying in the 1970s and on into the dawn of the 21st Century.

Your moment-to-moment interpersonal signals pull, fabricate, create the personal environment you inhabit.

The principle of self-determination states that your moment-to-moment interpersonal signals pull, fabricate, create the personal environment you inhabit. Don't blame your parents, your race, your society. Accept responsibility for your behaviors—which in turn elicits the response you get from your world. This point of view which seems so cliched today was shockingly heretical to the orthodox Freudian-Marxist determinists of the primitive 50's.

Reciprocal Relations

This reciprocal process by which human beings tend to pull from others responses that tend to maintain their limited security operations is what we mean by the *Principle of Self-Determination.*

Most statements describing what "others did to the sample case were worded so as to give responsibility to the subject. Thus we say, "He trained or provoked the group members to snub him," rather than "They snubbed him."

I have tried to stress the surprising ease and facility with which human beings can get others to respond in a uniform and repetitive way. Interpersonal reflexes operate with involuntary routine and amazing power and speed. The aggressiveness, obsequious fawning and shy withdrawal are some of the interpersonal techniques which predictably pull the reciprocal reaction from the "other one."

Your own interpersonal behavior has, more than any other factor, determined the reception you get from others.

Externalizing Blame

Human beings resist taking responsibility for their situations. This point of view plows headlong into the most widespread resistance. It threatens the most cherished beliefs of Western philosophy—from Sophocles—who stresses fate—to the modern mental hygienists—who overemphasize parental behavior. What is more important, it threatens the most cherished illusions of the average man who bases his security and self-esteem on the traditional procedure of externalizing blame.

No man...cuts another man's throat unless he wants to cut it, and unless the other man wants it cut. This is a complete truth. It takes two people to make a murder: a murderer and a murderee. And a murderee is a man who is murderable. And who is murderable is a man who in a profound if hidden lust desires to be murdered.

—D. H. Lawrence

What we are saying here to the human being is, "You are mainly responsible for your life situation. You have created your own world. Your own interpersonal behavior has, more than any other factor, determined the reception you get from others. Your slowly developing pattern of reflexes has trained others and yourself to accept you as this sort of person—to be treated in this sort of way. You are the manager of your own destiny. Attributing responsibility to the individual is what we called the "Principle of Self-Determination".

The Interpersonal Reflex

There are sixteen mechanisms or reflexes of interpersonal behavior which pull or provoke predicatable response from others. Of the sixteen mechanism, eight are adaptive and eight are pathological, each of which can manifest to a normal or extreme degree.

Adaptive

Pathological

Managerial
Autocratic

Manage, direct, lead   Guide, advise, teach

Provokes

Obedience   Respect

Extreme

Dominate, boss,   Seeks respect compulsively,
order   pedantic, dogmatic

Competitive
Narcissistic

Competing, assertive   Confident, independent

Provokes

Distrust   Inferiority

Extreme

Exploiting, rejecting,   Boastful, pride,
withholding   exhibitionistic

Aggressive
Sadistic

Frank, forthright,   Aggressive, firm actions
Critical actions

Provokes

Hostility   Passive resistance

Extreme

Attack, unfriendly   Punitive, sarcastic,
actions   or unkind actions

Rebellious
Distrustful

Realistic & justified rebellion,   Realistic weariness,
unconventional   skeptical

Provokes

Punishment   Rejection

Extreme

Bitter rebellious actions,   Acting hurt or suspicious,
complaining   distrustful

Self-Effacing	Masochistic
Shy, sensitive, modesty	Dutiful, obeying
Provokes	
Arrogance	Leadership
Extreme	
Anxious, guilty, self-condemning	Weak and spineless actions, submissive

Docile	Dependent
Respectful, admiring, conforming	Asking for help, trusting
Provokes	
Advice	Help
Extreme	
Over-respectful, docility, conforming	Clinging, begging for aid, depending on

Cooperative	Over-conventional
Agreeable, participating, cooperating	Affectionate, friendly
Provokes	
Tenderness	Love
Extreme	
Over-conventional, agreeing at all times , compromising	Seeking friendly feelings, effusive actions

Responsible	Hypernormal
Helpful, offering, giving	Supportive, empathetic, gentle
Provokes	
Trust	Acceptance
Extreme	
Takes responsibility, compulsively hypernormal	Pity, doting o,n soft-hearted

Chapter 6

Aim of Interpersonal Behavior

Previous theories of human destiny, all of European or Middle Eastern origin, stressed human submission to God or, in the case of Freud and Marx, to society. Our brash reference to "self-esteem," individual pride, was a patriotic attempt to bring American psychology in line with the Emersonian-Jeffersonian frontier ethos of our country.

Previous attempts to Americanize psychology—the Horatio Alger Myth, Dale Carnegie, the John Dewey approach—encouraged adjustment to the system, to the boss. Here, we stated flatly that your basic responsibility is to yourself. This became the cornerstone value of the 1960s hippies and the call to arms of the New Agers.

Your basic responsibility is to yourself!

The aim of interpersonal behavior was quite clear: "To ward off anxiety and preserve self-esteem." This notion that the aim of human behavior was to maintain self-esteem, which we defined as to feel good about oneself as an individual—became one of the major paradigms of the late 20th Century New Age Movement.

What Is Interpersonal Behavior?

Behavior which is related overtly, consciously, ethically, or symbolically to another human being—real, collective, or imagined—is interpersonal. This is a short but complex definition.

Let us consider some examples of human behavior in the light of this definition. The report from a reliable observer—"George insulted his father"—is clearly interpersonal. It tells how George related to his father and what he did to his father.

The aim of interpersonal behavior was quite clear: "To ward off anxiety and preserve self-esteem."

The finding "George says he is a friendly person" comes from a different observation point, the subject's self-description, but is still clearly interpersonal. It tells how George perceives his motives toward other people. Also interpersonal is the inference made on the basis of dream or fantasy material "George dreams that his mother is protecting him." This refers to a fantasized relationship between the subject and another person.

These descriptions of different aspects of the subject's behavior, which we call *protocol statements*, are the basic data on which we build a science of personality. They describe, at three different levels of observation, the subject's interpersonal relations.

Non-Interpersonal Dimension

Another dimension of personality is reflected in the statements "George acts impulsively," "George says he is not depressed," "George dreams of hatboxes." These descriptions are taken from the same three levels of observation—the outsider's report, self-

report, and dreams—but they are not directly interpersonal. Impulsivity, optimism, and a symbolic con-
cern with containers have figured in certain personality theories and have some importance in the understanding of personality.

Such descriptions are non-interpersonal because
they do not refer to the subject's relationship to other
people. They may be, and probably are, indirectly
interpersonal. If we investigate further we might learn
that George acts impulsively to impress others with
his strength, that he
says he is not de-   **You are the manager of**
pressed to prove that   **your own destiny.**
he does not need
psychotherapy, and that he has a vague childhood
memory of his mother bringing him lunch in a hatbox.
The non-interpersonal thus becomes interpersonal—
the personal characteristics take on a social meaning
and reflect his relationships with others.

Chapter 7

Survival Anxiety

Interpersonal behavior is crucial to the survival of the human being. From a second—and much more parochial—point of view, interpersonal behavior is the aspect of personality that is most functionally relevant to the clinician.

From the standpoint of human survival, social role and social adjustment comprise the most important dimension of personality. This is because of the unique biological and cultural aspects of human development and maturity.

Long Dependency

One of the major differences between man and the other animal species is his long and helpless infancy. Depending on the complexity of the culture, it takes from 12 to 25 years for a human being to attain developmental maturity. This long period of childhood and adolescence involves dependence on other human beings for nourishment, shelter, and security.

> Interpersonal behavior is crucial to the survival of the human being.

Many animal species, on the contrary, are ready to undertake complete responsibility for their own survival at birth, or shortly thereafter. In these cases instinctual methods of locomotion, food collection, and self-protection take over immediately. Rigidly built-in patterns of response are vital to their early self-sufficiency. Automatic physiological responses are the key to life for these infra-human organisms.

Relationships Key to Survival

The case of man is quite different. The human infant has limited physical capacity and few automatic behavior sequences for dealing directly with the physical environment. From the moment of birth, survival depends on the adequacy of interpersonal relationships. The water, warmth, and milk upon which the infant's life depends come from others. These primitive, basic transactions which the neonate carries on with others are, we are told, not rigidly fixed patterns. A variety of early parental response exists, and this is matched by a variation in neonate behavior.

This anxiety is dealt with—partially or completely, carelessly or lovingly, calmly or nervously—by the mothering-one.

Several experts in this field, including Sullivan, Klein, Erikson, Ribble, and Spitz, have claimed that the roots of personality are to be found in the earliest mother-child interactions. This claim is not surprising when we recall that a raw, intense, basic anxiety—concerned with the maintenance of life itself—may be felt by the neonate. And this anxiety is dealt with—partially or completely, carelessly or lovingly, calmly or nervously—by the mothering-one. The earliest kind of survival anxiety is, therefore, handled by interpersonal, social responses.

The Human Infant is Plastic

From the standpoint of physiology the human infant is not much different from any young mammal. From the standpoint of personality psychology, however, the human being at birth is an extraordinarily plastic, germinal nucleus with infinite potentialities for eventual differentiation.

It might be said that any neonate is a potential president, priest, poet, or psychotic. Personality psychology is concerned with the events and behaviors which determine the emotional and social development of the individual. The most important factors which account for the wide varieties of behavior characteristic of the human being are the interpersonal security operations which he develops and the social relationships—real and fantasized—which he integrates with others.

Primacy of Relationships

We have pointed to the crucial influence of the earliest social transactions between mother and child—crucial because of the survival anxiety involved and because of the complete dependence of the infant.

As the child grows, the primacy of interpersonal relationships does not lessen greatly. A seven-year-old child has developed many motoric patterns for self-protection, but on the hypothetical desert island or in any social context we cannot credit him with survival self-sufficiency.

The human being maintains existence by virtue of the long period of parental protection during which he assimilates the complicated cultural wisdom necessary for survival. This process of slow, and often painful, learning is intensely interpersonal.

Even at maturity, survival rests upon successful interpersonal patterns. The mutual dependence of mankind is inevitable. Whether we exist in a primitive tribe, a dictatorship, or an industrial democracy, the key to human survival lies in the adequacy of social interaction. Even the rare test case of a hermit falls within the limits of this generalization, since this adjustment technique always involves intense and often bitter "withdrawal" from others, and is one pattern of interpersonal reactivity.

The extent to which we automatically and implicitly demonstrate patterns of cooperation and submission to social demands—even in the most democratic society—is quite striking.

The extent to which we automatically and implicitly demonstrate patterns of cooperation and submission to social demands—even in the most democratic society—is quite striking. Failure to do so invites such real or fantasized threats to life that we automatically commit ourselves in countless ways to the interpersonal pressure of parents, societies, and contemporaries.

Reciprocal relations are more likely to develop with certain personalities. The principle holds most uniformly with pairs of symbiotically "sick" people. A phobic, dependent wife and a nurturant, strong husband would be such a pair. The more the husband takes care of her, the more the dependence repeats. The more the wife clings, the more pressure on the huband to be gentle and protective.

Chapter 8

Sickness Rules

I t is easy to accept that the successful, self-made person makes the grade and that humans strive and bargain for the interpersonal goals reflected in half the spectrum—independence, power, popularity, affection. It is often less comprehensible that humans should actively seek the other half of the circular continuum—dependence, weakness, distrust, and self-effacing modesty.

Why Provoke Rejection?

The question still remain: Why do human beings limit their machinery of social adjustment, manifest narrowed spectra of reaction and provoke a restricted set of reactions from others? Why do some individuals have no ability for realistic, modest self-criticism and compulsively express only narcissistic self-enhancing mechanisms instead? Why do others cling to retiring modesty and eschew the responses of proud self-confidence? Most puzzling of all to the occidental mind: Why do some of our neighbors masochistically court interpersonal humiliation—doggedly provoking rejection and isolation from others?

Sullivan Gives Answers

Harry S. Sullivan defines personality as the pattern of interpersonal responses employed to reduce anxiety, ward off disapproval, and maintain self-esteem. In general, humans experience less anxiety in a familiar situation, when employing familiar responses. Reciprocal relationships with crucial "others" develop quite naturally.

The more anxiety-provoking the individual's world—particularly his parental home—the more likely the person is to select the familiar, narrow, certain, response, and to avoid promising but uncertain potentialities. But the more an individual restricts hir actions to one narrow sector of the interpersonal spectrum, the more s/he restricts the social environment.

Personality is the pattern of interpersonal responses employed to reduce anxiety, ward off disapproval, and maintain self-esteem.
—Sullivan

The man who continually employs submissive reflexes tends to train people to boss him and thus discourage people from looking to him for forceful leadership. The submissive man's interpersonal world tends to become more and more lopsided, putting pressure on him to obey and not command. He thus comes to a restricted but stable relationship with his environment.

A normal, fairly flexible person can use any interpersonal response the situation calls for. S/he is less committed to, and less skillful, in the use of any particular reflex. So the sicker you are, the more power you have to determine the relationships you have. A maladjusted person with a crippled set of reflexes tends to overdevelop a narrow range of one or two interpersonal responses expressed intensely and often, whether appropriate to the situation or not. When two individuals interact, the "sicker" person determines the relationship.

> **When two individuals interact, the "sicker" person determines the relationship.**

The more extreme and rigid the person, the greater hir interpersonal "pull"—the stronger hir ability to shape the relationships with others. The withdrawn catatonic, the irretrievable criminal, the compulsively flirtatious charmer can inevitably provoke the expected response from a more well-balanced "other".

We meet here a lowest-common-denominator process, a Gresham's law of interpersonal collisions. Sick people control the interpersonal interaction. The "sicker" or the more maladaptively rigid, the more power to determine the nature of the relationship.

> **We meet here a lowest-common-denominator process, a Gresham's law of interpersonal collisions.**

The flexible person can pull a greater variety of responses from others—depending on hir conscious or unconscious motives at the moment. S/he can get others to like hir, take care of hir, obey hir, lead hir, envy hir, etc. The "sick" person has a very narrow range of interpersonal tactics, but these are generally quite powerful in their effect. In politics, however, the situation is more ominous. A country is a closed system, and you can't avoid the troublemakers—particularly since they usually have the weapons! Throughout most of human history, countries have been controlled by violent, suspicious, unpleasant men whose behavior would be considered criminal or psychotic if expressed in situations that they could not control by force.

Chapter 9

How We Get What We Bargain For

A patient poignantly reports: "I want a dependent, feminine mate, but my three ex-wives were bossy, exploitive tyrants." At the conscious level this man may "want" a feminine girl, but his behavior—immobilized, distrustful, and masochistic—forces the most neutral woman into exasperated activity.

Another patient states, "I want a strong, successful husband to take care of me; but all I attract are penniless artists and dreamy bookworms." This woman may consciously wish for a strong husband; but the strongest man would feel smothered and alienated by her automatic, deeply ingrained mothering reflexes—to which dependent men are drawn with mothlike fascination.

What human beings *consciously* wish is often quite at variance with the results their reflex patterns automatically create for them. Voluntary intentions, resolutions, even insights are feeble compared to the on-going 24-hour-a-day involuntary interpersonal reactions.

How a Poignant Woman Provokes a Helpful Attitude.

A woman reports to a psychiatrist a long list of symptoms, like insomnia, worry, depression and unfortunate events including divorce, unsympathetic employer, and so forth. Whether her expressions are scored separately or summarized, we derive a clear picture of a docile/dependent approach—"I am weak, unhappy, unlucky, in need of your help."

The psychiatrist is under strong pressure to express sympathetic, nurturant communications. Helpless, trustful behavior tends to pull assistance from other people. That is, dependency tends to pulls responsibility from the other. Of course, you don't have to be a rocket scientist to see that the patient-therapist situation lends itself easily to the "needs help/offers help" relationship.

What human beings *consciously* wish is often quite at variance with the results their reflex patterns automatically create for them.

There exists a tendency for the psychiatrist to express openly or as is much more likely, by implication in hir bearing, attitude, hir very quiet competence, that s/he knows how the patient can be assisted. Actually, the "nurturant interpreter/trustful follower" situation exists not in what the participants say but in what they do to each other.

The Penitentiary Trains the Prisoner for Criminal Aggression

Many cultural situations have interpersonal implications so built in that a flexible, collaborative relationship is impossible. In prison psychiatry, for example, it is virtually impossible to shake off the institution's implicit contempt for the inmate. Every nonverbal cue tells the prisoner that s/he is a dangerous, untrustworthy outcast. The prisoner often responds by accepting the interpersonal role s/he is being trained for. That is, narcissistic/competitive/sadistic approach pulls aggressive/rebellious/distrustful response.

> The recidivist criminal is least anxious and most self-confident when in passive rebellion against a strong punitive authority who feeds and beats him.

Long duration human relationships tend to be selective on both sides. Thus, the recidivist criminal is least anxious and most self-confident when in passive rebellion against a strong punitive authority who feeds and beats him.

Automatic Works

Automatic role relationships function to minimize anxiety, setting up smooth-flowing reciprocal interactions. When the pattern of interpersonal reflexes breaks down or is ambiguous, considerable distress generally results—manifested in symptoms of anxiety. For example, some prisoners are made uncomfortable by a guard who refuses to assume the authoritative role.

Symbiotic marriage partners can panic when the implicit assumptions of power, guilt, and dependence on which they rest are temporarily threatened. Factory, department store, office, university—all have complex networks of routine, unverbalized evaluation through which power, prestige, contempt, punishment, acceptance, etc., are expressed.

While I never researched it specifically, I suspect that people tend to select jobs and occupational roles in accord with their interpersonal techniques for anxiety reduction and self-esteem.

I suspect that people tend to select jobs and occupa-tional roles in accord with their interper-sonal tech-niques for anxiety reduction and self-esteem.

How Professor and Student Train Each Other

Professors are so addicted to the stereotyped teaching reflex that they often cannot inhibit the didactic response. One psychology professor's lecture developed the thesis that teachers should stimulate the student to seek answers himself: " Don't let them become dependent on you; make them think for themselves."

As soon as the lecture was over, a graduate student who had been well trained to the dependency reflex, rushed up with a question: "In my undergraduate teaching section, the students are continually asking me to solve their personal problems and demanding answers. What shall I do?" The professor responded, "You'll always find your students tending to trap you into solving problems that they should work out for themselves. *Now what I'd do* if I were you is…" As you can see, the verbal context of an interaction can be quite divorced from its interpersonal meaning.

Chapter 10

Interpersonal Reflexes

Interpersonal reflexes operate with amazing power. Many maladaptive subjects can provoke the expected response from a complete stranger in a matter of minutes! Chip-on-the-shoulder defiance, docile, fawning passivity, timid, anxious withdrawal can pull the reciprocal reaction from the "other one" with unfailing regularity.

Severe neurotics—defined at this level as individuals with limited ranges of reflexes—are incredibly and creatively skilled in drawing rejection, nurturance and so forth from the people with whom they deal. In many cases the "sicker" the patient, the more likely s/he is to have abandoned all interpersonal techniques except one—which s/he can handle with magnificent finesse.

This point of view plowed headlong into the most cherished beliefs of Western philosophy.

We say, "He trained or provoked the group members to reject him," rather than, "They rejected him." We take the subject as the focus of attention and as the focus of responsibility. This point of view plowed headlong into the most cherished beliefs of Western philosophy—from Sophocles who stresses fate, to the modern mental hygienists who overemphasize parental behavior.

Automatic Reflexes

In a large percentage of interactions, basic motives are expressed in an automatic reflex manner, so that they are often at variance with a person's own perception of them. This facet of behavior, often unverbalized and so subtle as to escape articulate description, is therefore difficult to isolate and measure.

Sometimes these interpersonal communications can be implicit. For example, Grandfather talks incessantly about the lack of initiative of modern youth in order to impress others that he is a successful, self-made man. Grandmother talks incessantly about sickness, calamity, and death to remind others that her time may be short.

Behind the superficial content of most social exchanges it is possible to determine the naked motive communications: I am wise, strong, friendly, contemptuous; as well as the concomitant messages: you are less wise, less strong, less likeable, contemptible.

Jung has described the "persona" as a mask-like front behind which more basic motives exist. We are dealing with similar purposive behavior, but in emphasis something more important than a social façade—closer, perhaps, to the "character armor" concept of Wilhelm Reich, or the "conversation of gestures" developed by George Herbert Mead.

Routine Reflex Patterns

The average adult is challenged, pleased, bossed, obeyed, helped, and ignored several times a day. Thus, the flexibly functioning person can demonstrate the sixteen interpersonal reflexes many times in any one day. A small percentage of individuals get "others" to react to them in the wildest range of possible behaviors and can utilize a wide range of appropriate reactions.

Many people, however, do not react with consistent appropriateness or flexibility. For example, one might respond to the pleasant stranger with a disapproving frown. Each person shows a consistent preference for certain interpersonal reflexes, while other interpersonal reflexes are very difficult for them to elicit or entirely absent.

Most people "train" others to react to them within a narrowed range of behavior patterns, and in turn show a restricted set of favored reflexes. Some people show a very limited repertoire of two or three reflexes and reciprocally receive and increasingly narrow set of responses.

Resistance to Change

These interpersonal automatic, involuntary nature reflexes, makes people most resistant to therapeutic change. The more the psychotherapy group members tried to explain to the subject why the person irritated them, the more s/he protested hir feelings of injury. Later, the person developed intellectual insight and cooperative, self-confident behavior, but during many months of treatment, spontaneous reactivity brought a return of the original responses.

The involuntary nature of these reflexes demands continual emphasis to keep them from slipping out of focus. This hidden dimension of behavior is so basic it is taken for granted. Con-

Interpersonal automatic, involuntary nature reflexes make people most resistant to therapeutic change.

sider this analogy: A physician may ask the patient to report any pertinent psychological events noticed during the previous day. The patient might remember a feeling of depression at the office, worry over bills in the evening. It is inconceivable that the person could report that s/he conveyed by gesture, bearing, tone of voice, and verbalization a consistent message of pessimism and resentment, and that the "others" the person regularly interacts with have been trained to respond to hir in an irritated and rejecting manner. Nor would the person be able to indicate that his ability to express tender or affiliative purposes is crippled and inhibited.

Chapter 11

Role Relationships

A person may be quite unaware of these spontaneous tendencies—to complain to hir spouse, be stern with hir children, boss hir secretary, depend on the office manager. When the person *consistently, routinely* favors certain mechanisms with one particular person significantly more than chance and tends to pull certain responses from that person to a similar degree, then a "role relationship" exists. In later years this phenomena was called "co-dependency."

Most durable relationships tend to be symbiotic. Masochistic women marry sadistic men—who tend to marry women who tend to provoke hostility. Dependent men tend to seek nurturant superiors, who in turn are most secure when they have docile subordinates to protect.

Take the oversimplified example of John who reacted to his wife with the reflex of grumbling reproach to an inappropriate extreme. His voice took on a tired, whiny quality the minute he entered the house. He could often be jolly, firm, or protective with his spouse, but as we piled up the thousands of interaction ratings, the trend towards mild complaint became increasingly clear. John did not *deliberately* inject the hurt, tired note in his voice, or

> ## Most durable relationships tend to be symbiotic.

plan the slight droop of the shoulders. He may not have been aware of the continuous mild passive irritation. It might take some weeks of therapeutic exploration for him to verbalize the private feelings for his bitterness: that he is a defeated genius whose wife caused his failure and he could be a success today if *she* had not persuaded him to marry and leave engineering school. More intensive analysis would, of course, trace the roots of these feelings back even further to genetic predispositions.

John is within essentially normal limits because he maintains a reasonably flexible range of interpersonal behavior. Over time, he would exhibit all sixteen reflexes. But he favored or overemphasized passive complaint and distrustful, hesitancy.

John entered a psyclotron—a therapy group—along with four other strangers. Over eight sessions, he lectured, argued, helped, cooperated, but the mechanism he spontaneously favored and manifested a significant majority of the time was passive resistance. At the same time, a summary was made of the fairly flexible interactions John pulled from the others. The group listened to him with respect, deferred to him, accepted his help, liked him, respected him, but *on the whole*, felt a mildly critical superiority in reaction to John's grumbling approach.

Duplicates Life Situations

In seven sessions of brief interactions, John succeeded in duplicating his life situation with four strangers. John, it must be remembered, is essentially *normal*. His wife and his friends, very likely, understand and adapt with humorous, although sometimes irritable, impatience.

The individual units of this behavior we call *inter-personal mechanisms* or *interpersonal reflexes*. These reflexes are automatic and usually involuntary responses to interpersonal situations. They are often independent of the content of the communication. They are the individual's spontaneous methods of reacting to others.

The exact manner in which these communications are expressed is complex. This much is clear: they are expressed partly in the content or verbal meaning of the communication, but primarily in the tone of voice, gesture, carriage, and external appearance. The interpersonal reflex is, therefore, not necessarily a conscious expression. It can be involuntary and not a deliberate or conscious performance.

The interpersonal reflex is not necessarily a conscious expression.

Two-Person Commerce of Communication

Reciprocal relations are probable, not inevitable. Aggression *usually* breeds counter-aggression. Smiles *usually* win smiles. Tears *usually* provoke sympathy. In specific cases, however, aggression can win tolerant smiles, tears can provoke curses. If you walk up and aggressively shove a stranger, the largest percentage will mirror your aggression—and probably shove back.

Your counter-response then becomes the issue. You might apologize, or retreat, but your statistically probable response is to shove back, perhaps harder. You have provoked a response which has reinforced your original action—shoving the stranger. This reinforcing process has been dignified with the title of the principle of reciprocal interpersonal relations. Interpersonal reflexes tend to initiate or invite reciprocal interpersonal responses from "others" that lead to a repetition of the original reflex.

Survival anxiety presses the individual to repeat and narrow down his adjustive responses.

The Pressure to Repeat Responses

Interpersonal activities are designed to avoid the greater anxiety. It might be said in general that the human being experiences less anxiety in a familiar situation than in a strange one, and less anxiety when employing familiar responses than strange ones.

Survival anxiety presses the individual to repeat and narrow down hir adjustive responses. The person thus comes to a stable but restricted reciprocal relationship with hir interpersonal world.

Pressure to Change

Yet the environment at large presents a person with a wide range of social stimuli. In any single day most individuals roaming around their ecological space find suitable situations for expressing all sixteen interpersonal mechanisms. To the extent that the individual inhibits some of these, the person is not employing the appropriate responses demanded by the environment. Failure to adapt to the world about it generally creates survival anxiety in the organism.

Dilemma

The human being is caught between two polar whirlpools of anxiety. Rigid repetition of interpersonal responses minimizes conflict and provides the security of continuity and sameness which Whitehead called "endurance".

But the environ-
ment does not remain
the same. Adjustment to
it demands a flexible
generality of interper-
sonal response. This

> Every scheme for the
> analysis of nature has
> to face two facts
> change and endurance.
> —Whitehead

leads to a critical survival dilemma—the basic conflict, if you
please, of human nature. To use Whitehead's words, "every
scheme for the analysis of nature has to face two facts *change*
and *endurance*."

This lead us to define two basic maladjustive factors in
terms of these dichotomous sources of anxiety: *rigidity*, which
brings a narrow adjustment to one aspect of the environment, and *unstable ocillation* which is an intense attempt to
adjust to all aspects of the presented environment.

Between the two maladjustive extremes of personality,
rigid continuity and oscillating non-continuity, occur the
greatest majority of human adjustments. Most individuals
tend to select a limited set of preferred reflexes which operate spontaneously, but not with inflexible repetition. The
average individual is still able to call out automatically any
and all reflexes along the continuum to meet the exigencies
of the environment.

In general orientation and in the crucial decisions of hir
life, a person is likely, however, to have employed the narrowed responses. And s/he has very likely succeeded in
training the significant "others' in hir life to react in reciproc-
ity to hir interpersonal style. The average person has thus
created hirself and hir world along lines of a purposive but
limited set of interpersonal relationships. The person has
worked out, usually by means of involuntary reflexes, a bal-
ance which is best calculated to meet the double threats of
rigidity and chaotic flexibility.

Chapter 12

Diagnosis of Experience

We each have an inner life of consciousness and an outer life of behavior. Consciousness is the blueprint for action. What we rarely are aware of, we rarely do. People will share their inner blueprints with you when it is reasonable, feasible, and relevant to their interests to do so. They are eager to collaborate, but reluctant to yield.

Philosophy of Internal and External

Western psychology has never satisfactorily resolved the tension between internal-subjective and external-objective phenomena. We have consistently imposed the method, language, and goals of the external upon the internal continuum. The two can be related only if their differ-ence is kept clear. First, we must distinguish between two different approaches to reality.

Consciousness is the blueprint for action.

Science is the study of movements, behavior, events external to the nervous system; the study of recorded movements and the communications of these movements to others.

People will share their inner blueprints with you when it is reasonable, feasible, and relevant to their interests to do so.

Art is the study of experience, events registered by communications systems within the body—the communicating of these experiences to others. Art can be just as precise, disciplined, systematic as the symbol systems of external science.

Existential-transactional therapy requires that the psychologist teach the patient to be a scientist in observing his behavior and an artist in describing his experience. Failure to distinguish between the recorded external and the naturally experienced internal leads to a variety of confusions.

Only external events—recorded behavior—can be part of a scientific—a game—contract. Internal events—sensory, somatic, cellular, molecular experience—require an explicit, artistic contract between the "one-who-turns-others-on" and the "one-who-is-turned-on". The patient must become an artist who care enough about the psychologist to turn-hir-on to hir experience.

The Outsider's View

When we set out to study consciousness and such elusive altered states as ecstasy, there is the observer's "subjective matter" and there is the subject's "reality" and usually these have no relation. The psychiatrist may see hebephrenic psychosis, when the subject may be experiencing hedonic ecstasy. The outside observer has an entirely different view from the experiencing person. The psychiatrist asserts it a "fact" that the subject sat in a catatonic state for two hours, refusing to talk, when the subject knows the "truth" to be that s/he was spinning far out of space-time into an ecstatic dance of neurons which made words inadequate and irrelevant. Of course, both are "right." But the conflict in perspective leads the patient to feel misunderstood, and psychologist to feel frustrated. Observer logic and neurologic cannot communicate. So the patient is committed to the mental hospital.

Inefficient Scientific Schemata

Science needs languages and measurement methodologies for external movements in space-time. Art developes detailed languages and methodologies capable of paying respect to the flowing complexity of the internal, the countless levels of neurological decoding, the many levels of consciousness.

In order to develop a science of behavior, our present schemata are inefficient because they confuse internal-external. They jumble together the evaluations of the experiencing scientist, with narrow measurements of the subject's behavior.

For example, three Parisian behavioral diagnosticians, Andre, Marcel, and Pierre, walking through the Bois de Boulogn, run across an undressed couple making lively movements on the grass. Andre, age 6, exclaims, "Look, they are fighting." Marcel, a sophisticated 8, replies, "Oh, no, Andre, they are making love." Pierre, a true Parisian at 10, adds, "Yes, and very badly, too." Empirical studies of psychiatric diagnosis suggest a similar difficulty in labeling and evaluating behavior in entrepreneurial terms.

Chapter 13

Diagnosis of Consciousness

There are as many levels of consciousness as there are neurological, sensory, anatomical, cellular, molecular, and atomic structures within the human body—a galaxy of communication systems, and energy patterns, being sent and received.

When psychologists set out to define levels of consciousness, they usually comes up with mental abstractions that tell only about their own trips. Thus, Freud defines the conscious as routine, conventional, normal awareness; the unconscious as unthinkable, naughty and repressed; the superego as highly valued. Freud is simply listing symbols of differing social meaning. Such listings differ from culture to culture. Our knowledge of consciousness, a biochemical process, must be based on our understanding of neurochemical process.

Before the discovery of the microscope, medicine was based on crude macroscopic observation. Before the discovery of neurotransmitter chemicals, psychology and psychiatry were in the same state. We are now able to define different levels of consciousness in terms of the neurotransmitters which produce them. We can study them systematically, and replicate our observations.

Where Is Your Head At?

Psychological diagnosis (except in the most administrative sense) cannot be carried out unless the diagnostician is aware of the level of consciousness—or combinations of levels—of the other. The diagnostic question is: "Where is your head at?"

This is a level of conscious description because it reflects how the subject chooses to present hirself and hir view of the world, It will be noted that we do not call it the level of consciousness, but of conscious communication. This is an important distinction.

The phenomena of consciousness is one of the most elusive issues in the history of Western thought.

It is impossible to obtain an objective evaluation of the subjective viewpoint of another person.

One of its most confusing aspects is, of course, its subjective nature. The scientist can never understand or measure what another person has in hir consciousness. It is often quite difficult for the subject hirself to know the focus and limits of hir awareness. Between the subject and the psychologist there exists any number of potentially distorting factors—deliberate omissions, expressive inaccuracies, and the like. And we never know the exact level of awareness from which the statements come.

Since it is impossible to obtain an objective evaluation of the subjective viewpoint of another person, many psychologists have attempted to discard the whole issue of consciousness. But in so doing an essential dimension of human behavior is lost.

Levels of Conscious-Intelligence

At our present crude and primitive level of understanding it is appropriate to consider eight levels of consciousness-intelligence.

1. *Autonomic nervous-system*: Mediating physiological satisfactions and warnings; pain-somatic-pleasure;

2. *Mid-brain:* Mediating mammalian emotion, aggression, territorial instincts, power, security;

3. *Left-brain* (dominant hemisphere): Mediating thinking, manual dexterity, language, symbolic learning, manufacture;

4. *Domestication-socialization circuits*: Mediating cultural behavior, sex-role-impersonation, moral-ethical behavior necessary for acceptance by society;

5. *Right-brain and sensory-somatic circuits:* Mediating awareness of body-function, rhythm, pattern, erotic-hedonic, aesthetic behavior;

6. *Meta-programming circuits:* Allowing consciousness of the brain as a bio-electric loom, fabricating realities;

7. *Neurogenetic circuits:* Permitting direct awareness of and communication with electronic-atomic information, e.g., brain-computer linkups;

8. *Frontal-lobe circuits:* Permitting direct awareness of and communication with electronic-atomic information, e.g., brain-computer linkups.

These levels are listed in order of the age, speed, power, complexity, expansiveness, and planful wisdom of the energy structure.

Each level of awareness can be *produced*. Each of these neural circuits can be turned on by neurotransmitter chemicals—naturally produced by or introduced into the body. Understanding this process brings us to chemical manipulation of our brain circuits with brain activating substances, which is the topic of another book in this series.

New Science of Psychology

The 20th Century may well find historical status as the epoch in which wo/man began to study hirself as a scientific phenomenon. This development, inaugurated mainly by Sigmund Freud around the year 1900, has brought about an impressive growth in the so-called humanist disciplines—psychiatry, psychology, anthropology, sociology. The hour is yet too early to begin writing the chronicles of our time, but certain trends, now clearly evident, allow tentative predictions.

Existential-transactional therapy requires that the psychologist teach the patient to be a scientist in observing his behavior and an artist in describing his experience.

I am convinced of the need for a science of psychology that is existential and transactional. By *existential* I mean a concentration on flexible concepts and methods that grow out of the unique changing situation. By *transactional* I refer to an open collaborative attitude between the psychologist and the person studied.

Exactly how can post-Einstienian ingenuity be applied to human problems? How can we use our brains to do good, to do good well, and to do good measurably well?

1. Why not study natural events as they occur, rather than artificial situations—like tests, experiments—arranged in our offices?

2. Why not use a conceptual language arising from the data rather than imposing upon the situation our own favorite prefabricated variables? We should be more flexible and eclectic in selecting concepts, recognizing the semantic "flimsiness" of verbal abstractions.

3. Since behavioral transactions are continually changing, why not continue to collect natural records throughout the term of the transaction? Why not expect our techniques and concepts to change as our subject matter changes?

4. Since behavioral transactions are not standardized, but always unique, why do we routinely rely on our own tests? Why not let the natural transaction produce its own records, which we can measure and interrelate? If and when the need for standardized tests grows collaboratively out of this natural situation, why not construct, revise, or design a measuring instrument for this unique situation?

5. Why ignore or blur the difference between consciousness and behavior? Why not develop maps, models, and measures for describing inner events and relate them to separate models and measures for describing external behavior? Imposing our favorite standards, concepts, and symbols on the situation is a form of intellectual narcissism that Western science has held up as the ideal.

I am implying rather a collaborative adaptation, a yielding to the unique data, a calculated and sensitive passivity to idiosyncratic facts. I suggest we select from the enormous storehouse of available verbal abstractions those that seem to fit the human situation we deal with. Let the situation determine the variables.

Transactional Research

Can we make our endeavor transactional, i.e., emotionally realistic? We must treat our fellow wo/man as what s/he is, a human being piloting a 30-billion-cell brain, and not as an object to be dissected manipulated, controlled, predicted.

The problem we study should not grow out of our own professional preoccupations, but should rather be a collaborative decision between the subject and ourselves. The patient helps define the variables. When feasible and relevant, the subject should help design and construct the record-collecting devices or test forms.

> We must treat our fellow wo/man as what s/he is, a human being piloting a 30-billion-cell brain, and not as an object to be dissected manipulated, controlled, predicted.

The subject should be treated as the phenomenological equal of the psychologist in the collaborative research. Patients, after all, are the world's leading authority on their own lives and the transactions in which they are involved. If we depersonalize patients, they will depersonalize us back. If we keep secrets from them, they will keep secrets from us. In the sort of research I am endorsing, subject and therapist, collaborators in the joint research agree on goals, and then both work to meet the forecasted standards.

Patient as Diagnostic Instruments.

By allowing the patient to react with others in a group therapy situation, s/he demonstrates, directly and openly, hir repertoire of interpersonal reflexes. Basically, the patient tends to accomplish hir own interpersonal diagnosis.

The therapeutic group serves as a small subsociety, a miniature world. Clinicians are not supposed to admit that they like, fear, or look up to a patient; their ratings, indeed, are supposed to be divorced from personal reactions. Naïve, untrained fellow patients do not "psychologize;" they generally judge each other in terms of their own direct reactions

> **Patients, after all, are the world's leading authority on their own lives and the transactions in which they are involved.**

Chapter 14

Sharing Space-Time

The diagnosis of interpersonal behavior is tremendously facilitated by the space-time location system. Here again we ignore tempting variables and focus simply on the basic questions: What space do they share? What time do they share? We thus define a powerful variable we might call intimacy, commitment, involvement, attitude, i.e., that angle of approach. We might hazard a definition of love as the amount of space-time shared.

We might hazard a definition of love as the amount of space-time shared

The first step in diagnosing behavior is to determine where the subject spends hir time, how long, how frequently, and with whom. Location in space-time is a relatively straightforward task and is basic to any psychological evaluation.

Power of Sharing Space-Time

The basic interpersonal issue is how much space-time will you share with another? Your office? Home? Bedroom? Body? What kind of time will you share? Day or night? By appointment only? The fact that the husband and wife spend thirty years together day and night is considered much more important than the emotional game they play—fighting, submitting, cooing, dominating.

If you want to change someone's behavior—share space-time with hir. Your space-time is the most valuable and potent instrument you have. If you understand this simple principle, you have attained a liberating direction of your life.

The basic interpersonal issue is how much space-time will you share with another?

Following this hypothesis we should expect that mother-child relationships—nine months of internal body sharing—and marital relationships—extended duration of internal body sharing—are the most potent change situations. College lectures and doctor-patient interviews are the least potent. This suggests that if you can't "mother" or marry them, the best way to influence behavior is to engage in reciprocal home visits or meet regularly in extra-work locations—bars, restaurants, beaches. The most successful programs for dealing with social "problems," like Alcoholics Anonymous, scrupulously avoid the power-loaded environment of the scheduled office interview.

Presence

Will the patient continue to come?

The first functional issue in behavior change is presence. Will the patient continue to come? How can we change hir if s/he won't share space-time with us?

In the prison, space-time factors become dramatically obvious. Consider a young "delinquent" sentenced to prison at age 19. Who is going to shape hir behavior? Other prisoners with whom the youth shares cell, meal, table, shop, bench, yard time—and often body space. Next to other convicts, s/he will share most time with guards. The middle-class professional calls the convict into the prison clinic for thirty to forty minutes a week. According to the space-time formula, such well-oriented interventions are pitifully limited.

Chapter 15

Self-Discovery Tool

A very powerful and ridiculously simple tool is thus available to the person interested in self-discovery. Humanist diagnosis involves the subject studying their own behavior. This leads to the practical conclusion: To change your behavior, start by changing your space-time locations. How you park your automobile body. My interpersonal relations could easily be changed by spending more time with my son, more time sitting on the floor looking up at others, and so on. Changes in consciousness must go along with alterations of behavior to avoid robotization.

Tune Your Own Behavior

Everyone makes their own interpersonal world. This was a radical notion in 1957. Our approach didn't urge adjusting to society. That was practically blasphemy because psychologists were suppose to help you to adjust—to better fit into the mold. We defined adjustment-maladjustment in terms of the individual, not

Everyone makes their own interpersonal world.

Judeo-Christian conformity or Freudian stoicism. Our radical advice was: Dial and tune your own behavior to get the results you want.

Behavioral Fingerprints

The most direct measures of interpersonal behavior would be based on continuous recordings of movements. For about one-tenth the cost of psychoanalytic sessions, one could tape twelve electrodes the size of a dime to one's body and obtain patterned readouts of one's muscular behavior that would produce profiles of one's behavior so unique, so precise as to be embarrassing—a *behavioral fingerprint.* There is no one in the world who uses throat plus hip plus hand-muscle movements like you. Psycho-physiologists don't provide us with these mirror-measurements because we're not ready to learn this much about ourselves—yet.

Gather a Sample of Behavior

For about one-tenth the cost of psychoanalytic sessions, one could tape twelve electrodes the size of a dime to one's body and obtain patterned read-outs of one's muscular behavior that would produce profiles of one' s behavior so unique, so precise as to be embarrassing.

So for practical diagnostic purposes it is useful to collect observational samples of behavior. For example, for a two-week period I carried a kitchen timer with me throughout the day. On waking in the morning I set it to ring every ten minutes and continued to reset it for ten-minute intervals until retiring in the evening.

Timothy's Behavioral Fingerprint

I collected observational samples of my behavior for two weeks by carrying a kitchen timer that rang every ten minutes. Each time it rang, I stopped and recorded my observations. Here is an example of how it works.

Time	Place	Movements	Posture	# Others	Other's Movements	Other's Posture	Game Index
9:30	bed	sleeping	lying	0			body maintenance
9:40	bathrm	washing	standing	0			body maintenance
9:50	bedrm	dressing	standing	0			body maintenance
10:00	kitchen	cooking	standing	4	eating	sitting	body maintenance
10:10	kitchen	cooking	standing	4	eating	sitting	body maintenance
10:20	bedrm	dressing	standing	0			body maintenance
10:30	car	going to church	sitting	3	going to church	sitting	religion
10:40	church	listening	sitting	35	listening	sitting	religion
.				.			.
.				.			.
.				.			.
4:00	son's rm	watching TV	sitting	1	watching TV	sitting	recreation
4:10	son's rm	watching TV	sitting	1	watching TV	standing	recreation
4:20	daughter rm	helping with homework	standing	1	homework	sitting	intellectual

The bell allowed a time-sample of my movements in space-time during each day. At each shrill jangle I entered on a sheet: (1) the time, (2) the place, (3) a description of my behavior, (4) my posture, (5) number of others present, (6) posture of others, (7) a code of my behavior according to a game-classification.

Such summary sheets reveal with humiliating clarity my behavioral characteristics during this period. In reviewing several days worth of summary sheets I noted that five times more units were spent with my daughter than my son—are my Oedipal factors operating? 60% of my posture involved a chair—hummm, chairman behavior? Power motives? 41% of the time was spent alone—indications of introversion? Alienation?

Be a Reality Groupie

The space-time—proximity—option implies that we should tell dissatisfied persons to hang out with people whom they emulate. Be a reality groupie. Tested by 4 billions years of unicellular evolution, the proximity principle works. You become like—absorb the characteristics of—the organisms you associate with. This is the unfailing law of personal reality creation. Imagine, for example, the change in your life if you were to hang out for three days with the President or the Pope or Elizabeth Taylor. Result #1: You would become a minor celebrity yourself.

Preality

Proximity determines your *Preality*—the reality you prefer, pre-fab, program. Think of your body as a Star Trek spaceship which you constantly propel into situations where no HuMan has gone before. But Preality

is not limited to physical proximity. Electric communication tremendously increases our Preality options.
If you could pick up the phone and
talk to the President or the Pope or   **Proximity**
Elizabeth Taylor anytime you **determines**
wished, the effects on your Preality **your**
would be profound.
                                       Preality.
Our Preality options are limited
by time. The change-agent simply
cannot share the amount of time necessary to alter
the movements of clients. Hours on the couch are an
inefficient and ineffective ploy. The behavior-
changer's role thus becomes that of a navigational
consultant helping the dissatisfied person understand
and get control of hir own proximity movements.

Chapter 16

Cyberpunks

Cyber means "pilot." A *cyberperson* is one who pilots hir own life. By definition, the cyberperson is fascinated by navigational information—especially maps, charts, labels, guides, manuals that help pilot one through life. The cyberperson continually searches for theories, models, paradigms, metaphors, images, icons that help chart and define the realities that we inhabit.

Cybertech refers to the tools, appliances, and methodologies of knowing and communicating. Linguistics. Philosophy. Semantics. Practical epistemologies. The ontologies of daily life. Words, icons, pencils, printing presses, screens, keyboards, computers, disks.

Typically, these time mavericks combine bravery, and high curiosity, with super self-esteem.

Cyberpolitics introduces the Foucault notions of the use of language and linguistic-tech by the ruling classes in feudal and industrial societies to control children, the uneducated, and the under classes. The words "governor" or "steersman" or "G-man" are used to describe those who manipulate words and communication devices in order to control, to bolster authority—feudal, management, government—and to discourage innovative thought and free exchange.

Who is a Cyberpunk?

Cyberpunks use all available data-input to think for themselves. You know who they are. Every stage of history has produced names and erotic legends for the strong, stubborn, creative individuals who explore some future frontier, collect and bring back new information, and offer to guide the human gene pool to the next stage. Typically, these time mavericks combine bravery, and high curiosity, with super self-esteem. These three characteristics are considered necessary for those engaged in the profession of genetic guide, aka counterculture philosopher.

Old World Cyberpunks

The classical Olde Westworld model for the cyberpunk is Prometheus, a technological genius who "stole" fire from the Gods and gave it to humanity. Prometheus also taught his gene pool to many useful arts and sciences. According to the official version of the legend, he was exiled from the gene pool and sentenced to the ultimate torture for these unauthorized transmissions of classical information. In an unauthorized version of the myth, Prometheus aka The Pied Piper, uses his skills to escape the sinking kinship, taking with him the cream of the gene pool.

The New World version of this ancient myth is Quetzalcoatl, God of civilization, high-tech wizard who introduced maize, the calendar, erotic sculpture, flute-playing, the arts, and the sciences. He was driven into exile by the G-man in power, who was called Tezcatlipoca.

Self-Assured Breed

Self-assured singularities of the cyberbreed have been called mavericks, ronin, freelancers, independents, self-starters, nonconformists, oddballs, troublemakers, kooks, visionaries, iconoclasts, insurgents, blue-sky thinkers, loners, smart alecks, Before Gorbachev, the Soviets scornfully called them hooligans. Religious organizations have always called them heretics. Bureaucrats call them disloyal dissidents, traitors, or worse. In the old days, even sensible people called them mad.

Cyberpunks have been called mavericks, ronin, freelancers, independents, self-starters, nonconformists, oddballs, troublemakers, kooks, visionaries, iconoclasts, insurgents, blue-sky thinkers, loners, smart alecks, hooligans, heretics, dissidents, traitors, even mad.

They have been variously labeled clever, creative, entrepreneurial, imaginative, enterprising, fertile, ingenious, inventive, resourceful, talented, eccentric.

During the tribal, feudal, and industrial-literate phrases of human evolution, the logical survival traits were conformity and dependability. The "good serf" or "vassal" was obedient. The "good worker" or "manager" was reliable. Maverick thinkers were tolerate only at moments when innovation and change were necessary, usually to deal with the local competition.

Cybernetic Society

In the information-communication civilization of the 21st Century, creativity and mental excellence will become the ethical norm. The world will be too dynamic, complex and diversified, too cross-linked by the global immediacies of modern—quantum—communication, for stability of thought or dependability of behavior to be successful.

The "good persons" in the cybernetic society are the intelligent ones who can think for themselves.

> **The "good persons" in the cybernetic society are the intelligent ones who can think for themselves.**

The "problem person" in the cybernetic society of the 21st Century is the one who automatically obeys, who never questions authority, who acts to protect hir official status, who placates and politics rather than thinks independently.

Chapter 17

Individual as Reality Pilot

The term "cybernetics" come from the Greek word *kubernetes*—"pilot." The Hellenic origin of this word is important in that it reflects the Socratic-Platonic traditions of independence and individual self-reliance which, we are told, derived from geography. The proud little Greek city-states were perched on peninsular fingers wiggling down into the fertile Mediterranean Sea, protected by mountains for the land-mass armies of Asia.

Psychogeography Rules

Mariners of those ancient days had to be bold and resourceful. Sailing the seven seas without maps or navigational equipment, they were forced to develop interdependence of thought. The self-reliance that the Hellenic pilots developed in their voyages probably carried over to the democratic, inquiring, questioning nature of their land life. The Athenian cyberpunks, the pilots, made their own navigational decisions.

These psychogeographical factors may have contributed to the humanism of the Hellenic religions that emphasized freedom, pagan joy, celebration of life, and speculative thought. The humanists and polytheistic religions of ancient Greece are often compared with the austere morality of monotheistic Judaism, the fierce, dogmatic polarities of Persian-Arab dogma, and the imperial authority of Roman (Christian) culture.

The Roman Concept of Director, Governor, Steersman

The Greek work *kubernetes*, when translated to Latin, comes out as *gubernetes*. This basic verb *gubernare* means to control the actions or behavior, to direct, to exercise sovereign authority, to regulate, to keep under, to restrain, to steer. This Roman concept is obviously very different from the Hellenic notion of "pilot."

It may be relevant that the Latin term "to steer" comes from the word *stare*, which means "to stand," with derivative meanings "place or thing which is standing." The past participle of the Latin word produces "status," "state," "institute," "statue," "static," "statistics," "prostitute," "restitute," "constitute."

Cyberpunk Pilots Replace Governetics-Controllers

The word "cybernetics" was coined in 1948 by Norbert Weiner, who wrote, "We have decided to call the entire field of control and communication theory, whether in the machine or in the animal, by the name of Cybernetics, which we form from the Greek for steersman."

The word "cyber" has been redefined in the *American Heritage Dictionary* as "the theoretical study of control processes in electronic, mechanical, and biological systems, especially the flow of information in such systems." The derivative word, "cybernate" means "to control automatically by computer or to be so controlled."

Society everywhere is in conspiracy against the self-hood of every one of its members. The most requested virtue is conformity. Self-reliance is its aversion. It loves no realities and creators, but names and customs. . . . Who so would be a man must be a nonconformist.
—Emerson
Nature

An even more ominous interpretation defines cybernetics as "the study of human control mechanisms and their replacement by mechanical or electronic systems."

Note how Weiner and the Romanesque engineers corrupted the meaning of "cyber." The Greek word "pilot" becomes "governor" or "director;" the term "to steer" becomes "to control."

Now we are liberating the term, teasing it free from serfdom to represent the autopoetic, self-directed principle of organization that arises in the universe in many systems of widely varying sizes, in people, societies, and atoms.

The Politics of Literacy

The etymological distinctions between Greek and Roman terms are quite relevant to the pragmatics of the culture surrounding their usage. French philosophy, for example, has recently stressed the importance of language and semiotics in determining human behavior and social structures. Michael Foucault's classic studies of linguistic politics and mind control led him to believe that

> *Human consciousness — as expressed in speech and images, in self-definition and mutual designation . . . is the authentic locale of the determinant politics of being. . . . What men and women are born into is only superficially this or that social, legislative, and executive system. Their ambiguous, oppressive birthright is the language, the conceptual categories, the conventions of identification and perception which have evolved and, very largely, atrophied up to the time of their personal and social existence. It is the established but customarily subconscious, unargued constraints of awareness that enslave.*

Orwell and Wittgenstein and McLuhan agree. To remove the means of expressing dissent is to remove the possibility of dissent. "Whereof one cannot speak, thereof must one remain silent." In this light the difference between the Greek work "pilot" and the Roman translation "governor" becomes a most significant semantic manipulation, and the flexibility granted to symbol systems of all kinds by their representation in digital computers becomes dramatically liberating.

To remove the means of expressing dissent is to remove the possibility of dissent.

Do we pride ourselves for becoming ingenious "pilots" and dutiful "controllers"?

Who, What, and Why is Governetics

The word "governetics" refers to an attitude of obedience-control in relationship to self or others.

Pilots, those who navigate on the seven seas or in the sky, have to devise and execute course changes continually in response to the changing environment. They respond continually to feedback, information about the environment. They are dynamic—alert—alive.

The Latinate "steersman," by contrast, is in the situation of following orders. The Romans, we recall, were great organizers, road-builders, administrators. The galleys, the chariots must be controlled. The legions of soldiers must be directed.

The Hellenic concept of the individual navigating hir own course was an island of humanism in a raging sea of totalitarian empires. To the East—the past—were the centralized, authoritarian kingdoms. The governors of Iran, from Cyrus, the Persian emperor, to the recent shah and ayatollah, have exemplified the highest traditions of state control.

The Greeks were flanked on the other side, which we shall designate as the West—or future, by a certain heavy concept called Rome. The caesars and popes of the Holy Roman Empire represented the next grand phrase of institutional control. The governing hand on the wheel stands for stability, durability, continuity, permanence—staying the course. Individual creativity, exploration, and change are usually not encouraged.

Chapter 18

Pilots of the Species

The terms "cybernetic person" or "cybernaut" return us to the original meaning of "pilot" and puts the self-reliant person back in the loop. These words—and the more popular term "cyberpunk"—refer to the personalization, and thus the popularization, of knowledge-information technology, to innovative thinking on the part of the individual.

According to McLuhn and Foucault, if you change the language, you change the society. Following their lead, we suggest that the terms "cybernetic person, cybernaut" may describe a new species model of human being and a new social order. "Cyberpunk" is, admittedly, a risky term. Like all linguistic innovations, it must be used with a tolerant sense of high-tech humor. It's a stopgap, transitional meaning-gernade thrown over the language barricades to describe the resourceful, skillful individual who accesses and steers knowledge-communication technol-

> **Cyberpunk is a risky term. Like all linguistic innovations, it must be used with a tolerant sense of high-tech humor.**

ogy towards hir own private goals, for personal pleasure, profit, principle, or growth.

Countercultures are sometimes tolerated by the governors. They can, with sweet cynicism and patient humor, interface their singularity with institutions. They often work within the "governing systems" on a temporary basis. As often as not they are unauthorized, like the ronin.

Cyberpuncks are the investors, innovative writers, technofrontier artists, risk-taking film directors, icon-shifting composers, stand-up comedians, expressionist artist, free-agent scientists, technocreatives, computer visionaries, elegant hackers, bit-biting Prolog adepts, special-effectives, cognitive dissidents, video wizards, neurological test pilots, media explorers—all of those who boldly package and steer ideas out there where no thoughts have gone before.

The Legend of the Ronin

Ronin is used by Beverly Potter in *The Way of the Ronin* as a metaphor based on a Japanese work for lordless samurai. As early as the 8th Century, *ronin* was translated literally as "wave people" and used in Japan to describe those who had left their allotted, caste-predetermined stations in life; samurai who left the service of their feudal lords to become masterless.

The ronin . . . has broken with the tradition of corporate feudalism. Guided by a personally defined code of adaptability, autonomy and excellence, ronin are employing career strategies grounded in a premise of rapid change. Ronin played a key role in Japan's abrupt transition from a feudal society to industrialism. Under feudal rule, warriors were not allowed to think freely, or act according to their will. On the other hand, having been forced by circumstances to develop independence, [ronin] took more readily to new ideas and technology and became increasingly influential in the independent school.

The West has many historical parallels to the ronin archetype. The term "free lance" has its origins in the period after the Crusades, when a large number of knights were separated from their lords. Many lived by the code of chivalry and became "lances for hire."

The American frontier was fertile ground for the ronin archetype. "Maverick," derived form the Texan word for unbranded steer, was used to describe a free and self-directed individual.

Although many of the ronin's roots . . . are in the male culture, most career women are well acquainted with the way of the ronin. Career women left their traditional stations and battled their way into the recesses of the male-dominated workplaces . . . like the ronin who had no clan, professional women often feel excluded from the corporate cliques' inside tracks, without ally or mentor.

Cyberpunks in the Soviet Union

The postwar generation of Soviets caught on that new role models were necessary to compete in the information age. Under Gorbachev, bureaucratic control was softened, made elastic to encourage some modicum of innovative, dissident thought!

Aleksandr N. Yakovlev, Politburo member and key strategist of the glosnost policy, described that reform:

> **We are talking about self-government, or self-sufficiency, and self-profitability of an enterprise, self-this and self-that.**
>
> —Yakovley

> *Fundamentally, we are talking about self-government. We are moving towards a time when people will be able to govern themselves and control the activities of people that have been placed in the position of learning and governing them. It is not accidental that we are talking about self-government, or self-sufficiency, and self-profitability of an enterprise, self-this and self-that. It all concerns the decentralization of power.*

Chapter 19

Examples of Cyberpunks

Christopher Columbus

Columbus was born in Genoa. At age 25 he showed up in Lisbon and learned the craft of map-making. This was the golden era of Portuguese exploration. Many pilots and navigators were convinced that the Earth was round, and that the Indies and other unknown lands could be found by crossing the western seas. What was special about Columbus was his persistence and eloquence in support of the dream of discovery. For more than ten years he traveled the courts of Europe attempting to make "the deal"—to find backing for his "enterprise of the Indies."

> **What was special about Columbus was his persistence and eloquence in support of the dream of discovery.**

According to the *Columbus Encyclopedia*, "Historians have disputed for centuries his skill as a navigator, but it has been recently proved that with only dead reckoning Columbus surpassed in charting and finding his way about unknown seas.

Columbus was a most unsuccessful governor of the colonies he had discovered. He died in disgrace, his cyberskills almost forgotten. At least that is what they tell us in the authorized history books.

In 1992 the Political Correction Department dismissed Columbus as a racist colonialist. The City of Berkeley struck down "Columbus Day" and replaced it with the official "Indigenous People's Day."

Mark Twain

Twain purchased a Remington typewriter when it appeared in 1874 for $125—which was a fortune in those days! In 1875 he became the first author in history to submit a typewritten manuscript to a publisher. **Twain was the first author in history to submit a typewritten manuscript to a publisher.** It was *The Adventure of Tom Sawyer.*

"This newfangled writing machine," Twain wrote, "has several virtues. It piles an awful stack of words on one page. It don't muss things or scatter ink around. Of course, it saves paper."

Mathias (Rusty) Rust

Rust, a 19-year-old loner from Hamburg, Germany, attained all-star status as a cyberpunk when, on May 28, 1987, he flew a one-engine Cessna through the "impenetrable" Soviet air defenses and landed in Moscow's Red Square. There were no gubernal or organizational motives. The technological adventure was a personal mission. Rust just wanted to talk to some Russians. German newspapers celebrated the event, calling it "the stuff of dreams," and comparing the youth to the Red Baron Manfred won Richthofen and Charles Augutus Lindbergh.

Ilya Prigogine

Ready for another Einstein? Well, here's a Nobel-prize-winning chemist who has freed us from the death sentence implied in the Second Law of Thermodynamics.

The task of presenting Prigogine to the nonscientific community was begun by Marilyn Ferguson in *Brain-Mind Bulletin*.

> *How did life develop in a universe of ever-increasing disorder? How do order and complexity emerge from entropy? Now Ilya Prigogine, a physical chemist, offers a startling explanation, complete with mathematical proofs: Order emerges because of entropy, not despite it!*

Order emerges because of entropy, not despite it!
—Prigogine

> *Open systems, in which a structure exchanges energy with the surrounding environment are what he calls "dissipative structures." Their form or pattern is self-organizing, maintained by a continuos dynamic flow.*

> *The more complex such a structure, the more energy it must dissipate to maintain all that complexity. This flux of energy makes the system highly unstable, subject to internal fluctuations—and sudden change. If these fluctuations or perturbations, reach a critical size, they are amplified by the system's many connections and can drive the whole system into a new state—*

even more ordered, coherent and connected. With each new state, there is greater potential for change. With new levels of complexity, there are new rules. As Prigogine puts it, there is a change in the nature of the "laws" of nature.

By showing how complex systems can arise from less complex ones, Prigogine helps bridge the gap between biology and physics, a contribution towards the unified field theory that Einstein sought vainly to find in his equations.

Neil Goodman

Most 19th Century physicists were highly conventional thinkers living in and influenced by Judeo-Christian monotheism: The barbarous notion that there is One-and-Only-One-God—a male, of course—who made the universe and rules over it like a Middle-Eastern sultan. God, or some other grim lawmaker, fabricated the universe out there. All that "mankind" can do is to decipher, step by step, what is already writ, passively examining the entrails of birds, performing scholastic translations of the great text of nature.

The problem with this servile approach to knowledge is that many different groups arise, each claiming to represent the One-and-Only, each demanding the right to destroy all others as heretics. Monotheists love ominous terms such as "external laws," and "laws of nature."

Quantum physics has changed all that. The philosophic implications of multiple realities have been thoughtfully discussed by J. A. Wheeler—the universe is preselected by consciousness; Nobel laureates Eugene Wigner and Brian Josephson—consciousness is at the root of the quantum prin-

The universe is preselected by consciousness.

ciple from which space-time-mass arise as secondary
structures; and Jack Sarfatti—the physicist is an artist
who molds atomic reality with the aesthetic integrity
of his intention. Popular books by Fritjof Capra and
Gary Zukav have demonstrated the correspondence
between ancient Oriental philosophies, especially Zen,
and the flux of quantum physics. The most probing
examination of the implications of multiple-reality de-
terminism has been provided by Harvard philosopher
Neil Goodman. Of Goodman, Howard Gardner, another Harvard psychologist, says

> *From Goodman's perspective, it...makes more sense
> to think of various characterizations of reality that might
> be presented in words, pictures, diagrams, logical propo-
> sitions, or even in musical compositions. Each symbol
> system captures different kinds of information and hence
> presents different versions of reality.*

> *In Goodman's view, works of art—like the models
> of physicists—can also be profitable viewed as samples.
> Just as certain fabric swatches accurately reflect the
> whole bolt, so may the fabric of life."*

The New Generation of Brain-Drug Researchers

Custodians of public morality denounce all drugs
as "escapes." From their standpoint, they are correct.
The Russians and Irish spend over a third of their in-
come on strong alcohols to escape brutal reality. Moral
custodians fail to understand that personal subjective
realities are, in many cases, superior to the grim social
rigidities.

The freer, the richer, the higher the quality of life, the more technologically advanced the culture, the more varied the brain-drug options available. In China there is no drug problem because there is no "problem" of individuality, or creative dissent. By contrast, in sophisticated centers where intelligent, creative, innovative people swarm together, you will find a gourmet range of botanicals and chemicals that activate the widest scope of brain circuits.

> The freer, the richer, the higher the quality of life, the more technologically advanced the culture, the more varied the brain-drug options available.

Today, the average suburban 18-year-old knows more about the brain-drug option than most sophisticated scientists did twenty years ago. More and more people are using more drugs with less furor and confusion and accident. The next rational step is to improve the chemicals so that they are safer and more efficient, more precise in duration, and brain-function activated.

A new breed of psychopharmacologists is producing new drugs that will provide the individual with fingertip access to and control of his own nervous system. There is no mental function or dimension of consciousness that cannot be intensified, accelerated, expanded.

Work on receptor sites and beta endorphins is isolating chemicals naturally produced by the body that simulate the effects of the most common "head" drugs like morphine or LSD. This research encourages the speculation that soon one can have one's blood typed or one's spinal fluid assayed to isolate and then synthesize precisely the chemicals that one's brain is geared to use as fuel.

Chakrabarty and Kennedy

Here is the ultimate step in active, confident, self-determination. Humanity is taking charge of the evolutionary process and writing the life script. No longer need we cower in helpless fear, victims of a blind genetic destiny. We can now create new forms of life,

A new breed of psychopharmacologists is producing new drugs that will provide the individual with fingertip access to and control of his own nervous system.

correct faulty DNA blueprints, use the amino-acid language of life to write the prescriptions preventing aging and death.

J. R. Chakrabarty and Ian Kennedy merit distinction because they have created *controversy!* It started when the Indian chemist, via recombinant DNA methods, created in the General Electric laboratory a new mutant bacteria that eats oil spills. His claim for a patent was turned down by the U.S. Government. Chakrabarty appealed and the Supreme Court in June 1980 issued its decision. Chakrabarty was legally credited as owning the life from he had created!

The Pope promptly denounced gene splicing as heretical and he was right. The Chakrabarty decision gave genetic engineers a license to set up their work—Brave New Life Forms. BNLFs!

Ian Kennedy is even more controversial. Working in a "safe" laboratory at U.C. San Diego, this British virologist cloned the semliki forest virus, although he had been given government permission to replicate only the sindbis virus.

The semliki forest virus is not dangerous. Dr. Kennedy surely knew this better than the federal officials who classify risk potentials. Four of Kennedy's graduate students exposed the existence of the unauthorized bacteria to the administrators. Kennedy hinted that the substitution of species might have been an act of sabotage.

An investigating committee suggested that Kennedy was guilty of a cover-up, and the brilliant researcher was barred from his own lab. Cover-up of what?

Kennedy exposed the most dangerous disease now troubling our species—bureaucratic, political interference.

Kennedy exposed the most dangerous disease now troubling our species—bureaucratic, political interference.

Roy Walford

When Roy Walford was a child, he pondered about the alleged invincibility of death. Being a thoughtful, intelligent, cub, he resolved to devote his life to the cure of this lethal disease. His studies in the histocompatibility locus antigen (HLA) system have "happily merged" with other work on the biology of aging: immunology, DNA repair, free radical biochemistry, and hormone studies.

Aging may be partially caused by a failure in the autoimmune system. You age because your immune system starts producing antigens against your own cells. In other words, you begin to reject yourself. Makes sense when you think about it! In September 1980, some researchers in the field of prolongevity began testing new antiaging drugs on themselves and their parents! When two developments occur in a science—(1) a convergence of many competing cures and (2) the experts dosing themselves—the breakthrough is usually close at hand.

Like other new-breed Smart Ones—cyberpunks—Roy Walford is a multi-disciplinary, wide-gauge thinker. He's sexually magnetic and that's apparently important. It's becoming clear that philosophers who can't master their bodies and esthetic energies can't help

> **Philosophers who can't master their bodies and esthetic energies can't help but give us a crippled world view.**

but give us a crippled world view. Like other cyberpunks, Walford has sysematically opened up his intuitive, relativistic right brain by means of the standard yogi techniques. Roy Walford made the future his home town.

Edward Wilson

Edward Wilson, distinguished Harvard biologist, was delivering a scientific paper at a meeting of the American Association for the Advancement of Science when a band of militant feminist academicians poured a pitcher of water over his head—as he stood by the lectern at a prestigious scholarly meeting.

Clearly, Wilson is doing something right. Anytime a young, respected, attractive frontier scientist gets mugged because of his data and theories, we're alerted to a Prometheus script.

This historical drama started with a romantic South African physician, Andre Marais, who, disillusioned with human behavior after the bitter Boer War, returned to the Transvaal and spent the rest of his life shooting morphine—from army supplies he had salvaged—while living with tribes of natives, troops of baboons, hives of bees, and colonies of termites. He discovered that a profound intelligence coursed through these alien societies. Their basic behavior patterns roughly duplicated in almost all respects the social behavior of humans. Indeed, these so called lower species had succeeded in solving many urban and territorial problems in the evolutionary cycle.

These successful species—the termites have been flaunting the same melodramatic lifestyles for 150 million years—seemed to be guided by some sort of collective genetic intelligence that uses individuals as preprogrammed units necessary for collective security. Individuals are apparently harnessed to their divisions of labor by means of imprinting that releases their specific innate mechanism.

Anytime a young, respected, attractive frontier scientist gets mugged because of his data and theories, we're alerted to a Prometheus script.

Now enter Edward Wilson, who writes a classic textbook on the behavior of social animals. We confront the notion of genetic intelligence, species planning, biological wisdom—heretical, vitalist, creativist notions that we considered in the Gaia section. There may not have been a genetic intelligence in the past, but there sure is now! It's us! The emergence of the science of sociobiology becomes an irresistible, irreversible multinational event. We become the genetic intelligence.

Once you start thinking at the level of species in-telligence, you raise your perspectives from personal realities to a broader space-time frame that makes the future the most exciting place.

We can start asking the simple but powerful navi-gational question: Where is evolution taking our spe-cies? The answer is: In any direction, fashion, style, mode that we—led by the New Scientists—choose.

Chapter 20

The Cyberpunk as Role Model for the 21st Century

The tradition of the "individual who thinks for hirself" extends to the beginnings of recorded human history. Indeed, the vary label of our species, *Homo sapiens*, defines us as the animals who thinks. If our genetic function is computare—to think, then it follows that the ages and stages of human history, so far, have been larval or preparatory. After the insectoid phases of submission to gene pools, the mature stage of the human life cycle is the individual who thinks for hirself. Now, at the beginning of the information age, are ready to assume our genetic function?

The cyberpunk person, the ronin, the pilot who thinks clearly and creatively, using quantum-electronic appliances and brain know-how, is the newest, updated, top-of-the-line model of the 21st Century: *Homo sapiens cyberneticus.*

Let Science Rule

Every branch of science currently is exploding with theories, techniques, and discoveries that dramatically change our concepts of the universe. I hope that by writing this PR puff for scientific intelligence, I can contribute to the recognition of those upon whom our future rests. Because the grim bottom line is this: Science and only science can solve the problems of the past and produce the improved future.

Let's put it bluntly: Scientists should stop shirking their responsibility and take charge of human affairs. When we were territorial primates we were naturally led by barnyard politicians.

We now understand that spaceship Earth is a delicate, complex web of energy processes that must be understood and harmonized if we are to survive. Politics has become too important to be left **We would not let the controls of a 747 fall into the hands of a congressman.** to politicians who cannot and will not comprehend the situation. Our rulers in the future must be people with scientific training and with brains wired to handle relativistic complexity. We would not let the controls of a 747 fall into the hands of a congressman. Our officials should be selected the way our athletic teams are chosen—on the basis of recorded performance, of demonstrated excellence.

The Cyberpunk Code:

- Think for yourself
- Question Authority
- Just Say Know

Printed in the USA
CPSIA information can be obtained
at www.ICGtesting.com
JSHW012056140824
68134JS00035B/3471